VICTORIAN ARCHITECTURE AND FURNITURE

VICTORIAN ARCHITECTURE AND FURNITURE

Grange BOOKS

A QUANTUM BOOK

Published by Grange Books
an imprint of Grange Books Plc
The Grange
Kingsnorth Industrial Estate
Hoo, nr. Rochester
Kent ME3 9ND

1-84013-283-3

This book is produced by
Quantum Books Ltd
6 Blundell Street
London N7 9BH

Project Manager: Rebecca Kingsley
Project Editor: Judith Millidge
Designer: Wayne Humphries
Editor: Clare Haworth-Maden

The material in this publication previously appeared in
Introduction to Victorian Style, Encyclopedia of Furniture

QUMVA&F
Set in Times
Reproduced in Singapore by Eray Scan (Pte) Ltd
Printed in Singapore by Star Standard Industries (Pte) Ltd

8.95

CONTENTS

INTRODUCTION

T

The meaning of what it was to be a Victorian was as complex then as it is now. Today it does not simply describe a period in history, the 64-year reign of a queen from 1837 to 1901. For while 'Tudor' and 'Georgian' are evocative of phases in British history, 'Victorian' has entered the English language as a rich adjective that describes more than the past. 'Victorian' now rings of strict morality, solemnity, Christian ethics, ideas about individual industry coupled with responsibility to the community and, above all, conventionality.

Opposite: Queen Victoria, painted by Franz Xavier Winterhalter in 1859.

Below: The Machinery Court of the Great Exhibition, situated in the central aisle, included the 'Great Hydraulic Press' used in 1849 for the construction of the Britannia tubular bridge over the Menai Straits.

For H Stannus and other contemporary eulogists for late-nineteenth-century British culture the word 'Victorian' was synonymous with progress. In his 1891 study of the life and work of the artist Alfred Stevens, Stannus wrote of '. . . our peculiarly modern or VICTORIAN style'. Yet Matthew Arnold, in his book *Culture and Anarchy* of 1869, equated the upper reaches of Victorian society with barbarism and the middle classes with philistinism.

VICTORIAN VALUES

Victorian values did not come into being with the accession of Victoria to the throne in 1837, nor did they end in 1901 on her death. Just as they were displayed in the activities of figures such as Hannah Moore, the evangelising philanthropist, in the first years of the nineteenth century, the early twentieth century saw the continuity of the same concerns.

Victorian values, however, were not firmly entrenched until the late 1840s and were already breaking down by the 1870s. This is the age that has come to be known as the 'High Victorian' period. These years saw the height of British economic dominance, intense innovative activity in industry and communications and the untrammelled growth of the British Empire. In the 1870s Victorian Britain went through the first of a series of crises of

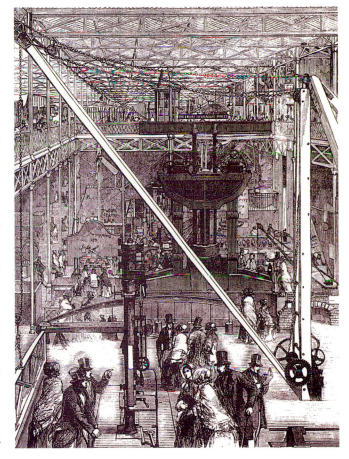

confidence: social investigators told of the extent of deprivation in her cities, while the scramble for colonies in Africa by her European rivals disturbed the nation's confidence in the British Empire and the economies of those same countries were clearly developing at a faster rate than Britain's. A new generation, which did not share their parents' beliefs, came to regard the term 'Victorian' with scorn.

VICTORIAN ART AND DESIGN

The same trends can be recognised in Victorian art and design. The most significant works of the art, craft and industry of the High Victorian period were, in essence, celebrations of Victorian culture. Even ordinary, day-to-day items found in Victorian homes echoed the values found in greater society. The rise of the Gothic style in mid-nineteenth-century Britain, which penetrated the homes of all classes, was for its proponents a highly moral style, reflecting hard work and craftsmanship.

The decades after 1870, however, saw the ascendancy of designers and artists, primarily the members of the Arts and Crafts Movement, who used their work to issue a challenge to Victorian morality, propriety and taste.

EARLY VICTORIAN STYLE

The strains of Classicism which had dominated taste in the first quarter of the century, the 'Regency' style, slowly began to go out of fashion. This style was typified by the highly

Below: Despite its prosaic function, the first letter box, set up at Ludgate Circus in London in 1855, was ornamented and surmounted by a ball finial.

POST OFFICE
LETTER BOX
Nº 1

MILES FURLONGS YARDS
3   213
FROM THE GENERAL POST OFFICE

regimented and restrained 'Greek' terraces surrounding Regent's Park in London, designed by John Nash. The Victorian mind, seeking novelty and exoticism, was not satisfied with this neo-Georgian Classicism: terraces of uniform white façades and rooms tastefully decorated with pale friezes depicting tales of Greek mythology and furnished with Chippendale chaises longues, Wedgwood vases and Hepplewhite cabinets.

Even Nash, the leading architect of the Regency period, bowed to this restlessness with 'good taste' by extending and improving William Porden's Royal Pavilion in Brighton

Below: 1840s' summer fashions paraded against the Neo-Classical backdrop of Cumberland Terrace, Regent's Park, in London.

SUMMER FASHIONS for 1840, by B. READ & Cº 12, Hart Sᵗ Bloomsbury Sqᵗ LONDON, & Broad Way, New York, AMERICA.

Right: Ornament triumphs over design in this Minton potpourri. The handles are derived from the eighteenth-century vogue for chinoiserie.

Below: The Hope Vase (1855), designed for Henry Thomas Hope by Louis Constant Sevin and carved by J V Morel, is a blend of Rococo fantasy and Neo-Renaissance ornamentation.

in the style of an Indian palace during the second decade of the century. This amazing building prefigured Victorian fashions in architecture and design in its Chinese and Gothic details and the use of structural cast iron. (But it should nevertheless be remembered that the taste for Classical art and design never completely disappeared during the Victorian period.)

THE INFLUENCE OF FRANCE

Under the influence of Paris and 'Le Style Empire', French fashions dominated British style in the 1830s and 1840s. This can be seen most directly in the Rococo Revival, which men like Benjamin Dean Wyatt, the architect and son of James Wyatt, promoted as a grand style, befitting the status of the increasingly grand British Empire.

THE ROCOCO STYLE

The Rococo style originated in France in the 1730s and by the second half of the eighteenth century was used as a term to describe the European fashion for rich ornamentation, often in the form of marine and floral motifs, scrolling and curvilinear designs. Widely regarded as a frivolous style, Rococo broke all the rules of Classical good taste: symmetry, balance, geometrical order and architectonic decoration. In all areas of the decorative arts, it was characterised by flights of fancy, *trompe l'oeil*, illusionary construction and, above all, ostentatious decoration.

The sources of the mid-nineteenth-century Rococo Revival in Britain are to be found in the popularity of floral ornamentation in the 1820s, promoted by firms such as Gillows of London and Lancaster. The firm decorated its furniture with rich acanthus ornament and lavish scrolled carving. The fashion for

Rococo design had been stimulated by the availability in London of items of furniture displaying the very high standards of French craftsmanship after the Revolution.

The origins of the Rococo Revival in Britain were aristocratic. In 1834 the Duchess of Rutland, for example, employed Benjamin Dean Wyatt to redesign Belvoir Castle, in Leicestershire, in the Louis XIV style. But the Rococo Revival at its height – in the 1840s – was a solidly bourgeois affair. Numerous manufacturers used the Rococo style to give their products an air of expensive elegance. These goods were not historical recreations of eighteenth-century designs but generalisations of Rococo characteristics: 'C' and 'S' scrolls, naturalistic ornamentation, cabriole (double-carved) legs, balloon backs, deep upholstery and curvilinear forms.

Although no longer in the vanguard of fashion by the mid-1850s, Rococo continued to be a popular decorative style. It was an excellent vehicle for the bourgeoisie to display its wealth and taste and has consequently been identified as the worst example of Victorian excess by twentieth-century historians of applied art.

ROCOCO FURNITURE

The kind of furniture now seen as typically 'Victorian' originates from this mid-nineteenth century Rococo Revival. A button-backed, deeply upholstered armchair in a richly coloured velvet and with curved walnut legs is as much a symbol of the Victorian era as

Right: This ornamental Minton vase of tinted Parianware overlaid with exquisitely fashioned passionflowers and foliage in decorative relief was manufactured in 1854.

Below: This naturalistically painted jug and matching glass were produced by Richardson of Stourbridge, one of the more progressive glassmakers of the mid-nineteenth century and a frequent collaborator with Felix Summerley, alias Henry Cole.

the Albert Memorial.

The apparent luxury and excess of Rococo became available to the poorer classes with developments in furniture-making and decorative techniques. The firm of George Jackson and Sons produced a kind of putty which could be modelled, painted and then gilded on site to give the appearance of skilfully carved wood for a quarter of the cost. Similarly, the development of *papier-mâché* furniture encouraged highly moulded Rococo forms, such as cabriole legs, previously the products of costly craftsmanship.

THE SEARCH FOR A VICTORIAN STYLE

By the middle of the nineteenth century questions of style were perplexing Victorian designers and intellectuals. British art and design was widely regarded as being second rate when compared to the French decorative arts of the period. Styles originating in Paris were held up in London to be the zenith of artistic achievement.

Writers, intellectuals, designers and manufacturers argued that Britain, with its commercial superiority and Christian morals, ought to produce art and design worthy of its achievements in commerce and industry rather than plagiarising those of her rivals.

THE SCHOOL OF DESIGN

In 1835 the Select Committee of Arts and Manufactures, formed under Robert Peel's government to investigate this very problem, came to the conclusion that state-sponsored schools of design should established so that their graduates could be employed by industry to improve the standards of design and ornamental decoration. The first of these schools was founded in 1837 in Somerset House in London and by the mid-1840s 11 new provincial branches of the School of Design had been set up.

HENRY COLE

During these years, Henry Cole, a senior civil servant, was addressing the same problem of raising the standards of design. He believed that the best way to improve Victorian design and public taste would be to persuade industry to employ fine artists. To bring art to the manufacturing industry, in 1847 he launched a company which he called Felix Summerley's Art Manufactures. Cole (under the pseudonym of Felix Summerley) acted as an entrepreneur, commissioning designs from renowned artists and persuading manufacturers to use them.

THE COLE GROUP

Through the School of Design and Felix Summerley's Art Manufactures there emerged a core of artists, designers and intellectuals linked to Cole. The key figures in the 'Cole Group' were John Bell, Richard Redgrave, William Dyce, Daniel Macliese, Matthew Digby Wyatt, Ralph Nicolson Wornum, Gottfried Semper and George Wallis.

The Cole Group became the design establishment of mid-nineteenth century Britain. It wished to bring a rational influence to bear upon Victorian style, arguing through its mouthpiece, the *Journal of Design and Manufactures*, for simplicity over complexity.

PRINCE ALBERT AND THE GREAT EXHIBITION

The most eminent of Cole's collaborators was Queen Victoria's husband, Prince Albert of Saxe-Coburg-Gotha. In his capacity as president of the Royal Society of Arts, the Prince Consort attempted to promote the application of art to industry. In 1847 he and Cole planned

Left: Prince Albert, Queen Victoria's consort and a noted patron of the arts.

Below: This drawing, published by the Illustrated London News *in June 1850, gives some idea of the vastness of Paxton's great Crystal Palace, situated between Rotten Row and Carriage Road in London's Hyde Park.*

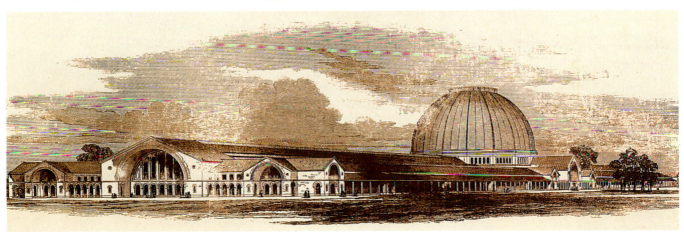

a number of annual didactic exhibitions with the specific intention of raising standards of taste. These smaller displays led the way to an immense one: London's Great Exhibition of the works of industry of all nations in 1851, housed in Joseph Paxton's 'Crystal Palace'.

Despite the fact that the Great Exhibition of 1851 was dominated by the Rococo Revival, it marked the first major Victorian attempt to break free from the dominance of French trends in taste and to search for a truly Victorian style.

POPULAR VICTORIAN TASTE

To Henry Cole, the exhibition was a disappointment, for his hopes of finding a union between art and industry had not been met. The critics lashed out at the use of excessive ornamentation, the out-and-out historicism and the absurdity of the majority of the exhibits. But the most popular exhibits, and frequently those that incurred the critics' wrath, were the ones that displayed the most ostentatious ornamentation and that were the most historicist.

The same values and qualities so prized by visitors to the Great Exhibition were echoed in the furnishing and decorative predilections of middle-class Victorians. They liked their furniture to be ostentatious and conspicuous, emphasising surface over structure and display rather than rational construction. The middle decades of the nineteenth century saw the dominance of veneering, graining, ormolu, gilding, embossing, chasing and many other forms of decorative treatment.

Although widely associated with Victorian architecture, historicism also dominated the decorative arts. Greek, Roman, Gothic, Egyptian and other historical styles provided rich sources of inspiration which manufacturers could plunder at will.

Bottom: Minton, whose display of plant pots and jardinières is featured here, was an exhibitor at the Great Exhibition.

Below: An aerial view of the formally titled 'Palace of Industry for all Nations', as seen from Kensington Gardens.

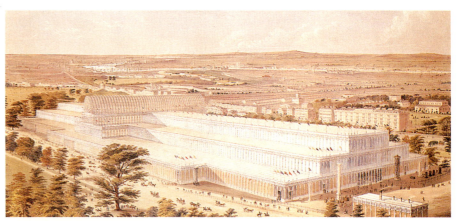

VISUAL PUNS

The Victorians were also fond of *trompe l'oeil* effects, particularly if they simulated expensive materials. Glass was painted to look like marble and zinc was electroplated to make it indistinguishable from sterling silver to the untrained eye.

Victorians liked their objects to contain narrative devices. Mottoes, pithy sayings and psalms were engraved into metalwork, stitched into fire screens and cushions and carved into chair backs. A Rococo-style chair from Dublin shown at the Great Exhibition, for example, with carved dogs for arms, had carved across its back the legend: 'Gentle when stroked, angry when provoked'.

OSTENTATION

The rising middle classes, prosperous on incomes from commerce and industry, were keen to display their wealth. Drawing rooms were brimming with armchairs, sofas, chaises longues, rich curtains, thick-pile carpets and

so on. Their concern was usually not with the patronage of craftsmanship or art, or the cultivation of a knowledge of the antique, but with the overt display of fashionable taste. Manufacturers responded by developing techniques for mass producing furniture, ceramics and metalware. Machine-carving, anathema to the purist, allowed the furniture industry to create pieces with the scrolling and turned balusters of handcrafted masterpieces at a fraction of the price.

THE VICTORIAN STYLE RE-EVALUATED

Despite the receptivity of popular taste to the new, the novel and exotic, the Victorian period has frequently been maligned as a low point in the history of style. The story of art and design in much of the twentieth century has been written by men and women inspired by the values of Modernism. Nikolaus Pevsner's *Pioneers of Modern Design*, for instance, dismisses nineteenth-century preferences for extravagant ornamentation, narrative devices,

Above: An electroplated tureen designed in 1880 by Christopher Dresser for Hukin & Heath of Birmingham.

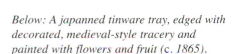

Left: A painted and gilded lacquer box decorated with an inset view of Paxton's Crystal Palace.

Below: A japanned tinware tray, edged with decorated, medieval-style tracery and painted with flowers and fruit (c. 1865).

trompe l'oeil, sentimentality and decorative novelty as 'bad taste'.

But it is interesting to note that as the dominance of Modernism in culture has withered away, Victorian art and design has become the subject of increasing attention. The values in art and design that the Victorians held so dear correspond with those that Post-Modernists prize today. Just as Owen Jones sought eclecticism in his sweeping survey of the styles of all periods and places, *The Grammar of Ornament* (1856), so many modern designers are today celebrated for very similar enthusiasms.

Certain figures, such as the architect Lewis Cubitt, have been ascribed roles of great importance. During the reign of Modernist architectural thought a building such as Charles Barry's Houses of Parliament, a nineteenth-century edifice decorated in the architectural style of the Middle Ages, the Gothic, was considered the height of irrationality. With the rise of Post-Modernism, this building is now regarded as an important part of Britain's architectural heritage.

ABOUT THIS BOOK

Far from being an obvious and easily definable expression of the aspirations of a dominant culture, style in the Victorian age was thus a battleground: arguably the first real style wars were being fought at the Great Exhibition. Focusing on the architecture and furniture of this period, this book details the many styles that both individually and together have come to be regarded as exponents of the 'Victorian style', including Neo-Classicism, the Rococo Revival, the Renaissance Revival, the 'Queen Anne' style and the High Victorian Gothic.

Left: This elegant, spun-glass fountain decorated with birds was made in Stourbridge, c. 1900. Wax fruit and stuffed animals were also popular items similarly encased within glass domes.

Below: The 27-foot- (8.23m-) high crystal fountain manufactured by F & C Osler, located in the centre of the building, was greatly admired by Queen Victoria at the Great Exhibition.

A PROLIFERATION OF DESIGNS AND STYLES

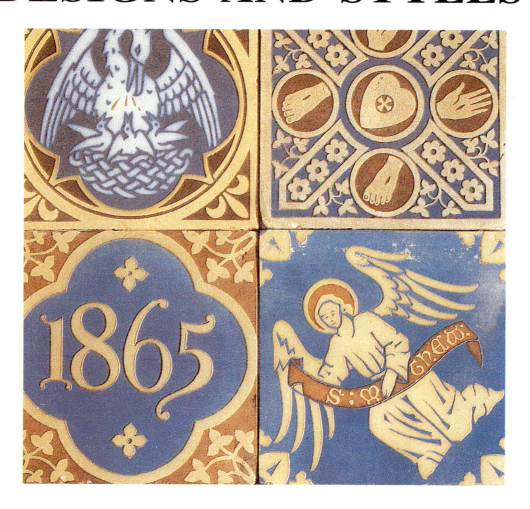

Preceding page: These Victorian tiles are decorated with medieval Christian motifs.

Below: The Elgin Vase, with its delicately etched Classical motifs and running frieze, was completed by John Northwood.

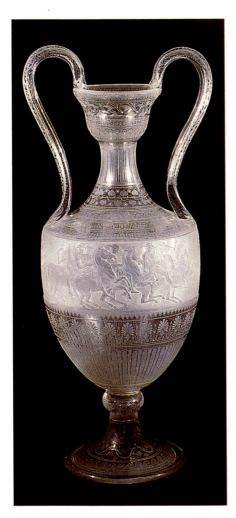

Victorians placed huge importance on style. Their edifices and artefacts were seen to be made attractive, fashionable and meaningful by being cloaked in historical decoration and ornament. Even the most functional things were disguised in this manner: water works were dressed up as Greek temples and sewing machines as painted *objets d'art*, for example.

NEO-CLASSICISM

The story of Neo-Classicism in the nineteenth century can be traced back to the Palladianism of William Kent in the early eighteenth century. Its development was also influenced by James 'Athenian' Stuart in the 1760s, who was notable for his Spencer House and book *Antiquities of Athens* (1762). In the 1760s, Stuart was succeeded in his position of eminence by Robert Adam, whose calm, elegant variant of Classicism, inspired by Pompeii, led fashionable taste until the 1780s. He in turn was superseded by James Wyatt, whose allegiance to Classical idioms was erratic and who produced his most famous buildings in the Gothic style, such as Lee Priory in Kent.

Around the turn of the century, the interest in Classicism, which had until that point been diverse in character, took on a particularly Greek aspect, with men like Thomas Hope arguing for Greek over Roman orders. The installation of the Parthenon sculptures in the British Museum in 1816, brought back by Lord Elgin in 1806, fuelled the interest in Neo-Classicism. The style peaked in the first decades of the century, but the taste for Neo-Classicism, or 'the Greek', as contemporaries referred to it, had declined by Victoria's accession to the throne in 1837. This is usually characterised as a revolt against the 'good taste' of Chippendale furniture and Nash terraces and a desire for novelty and 'flights of fancy' exemplified by the bizarre tastes on display at the Great Exhibition.

But Neo-Classicism continued to exert an influence on Victorian art and design until the 1860s, when many of its leading proponents died, including the sculptor John Gibson (in 1866) and Sir Robert Smirke, the architect (in 1867).

THE VICTORIAN RENAISSANCE REVIVAL

British artists and designers, since the age of the Grand Tours, had looked to Italy for inspiration. Accordingly, the Victorian period was not exempt from the influence of the Italian Renaissance and many of the best late-nineteenth-century paintings show it. In fact, it is difficult to distinguish a particular revival, for the Italian Renaissance proved to be a perpetual influence on Victorian artists and designers. Interest was stimulated in the Italian Renaissance by some of the greatest works of art-history scholarship, among them John Ruskin's *Stones of Venice* (1849) and Walter Pater's *The Renaissance* (1873).

The style was preferred by the mid-Victorian design establishment, the Prince Consort and the Cole Group; it was also the architectural preference of the political establishment of the day. A number of prestigious schemes resulted in Renaissance-style buildings and even the Gothic architect William Burges, under pressure from his client, produced a Renaissance-style Worcester College in Oxford in 1864.

ALFRED STEVENS

Two groups of artists and designers were considerably influenced by the Italian Renaissance. The first was the circle of designers and theorists around Prince Albert and Henry Cole. Cole was instrumental in the appointment of the most important revivalist, Alfred Stevens, to the School of Design in 1845, where he was employed to teach 'drawing and painting, ornament and geometrical drawing and modelling'. In 1850 Stevens left London and the School of Design and moved to Sheffield, where he was employed by the iron-founder Henry E Hoole and Company, which exhibited his designs at the Great Exhibition. He was also employed by Minton and Company, the ceramic manufacturers, to produce a series of vases and plates.

His first major success was as a sculptor,

Left: The British Neo-Classical sculptor John Gibson (1760–1866) studied under both Flaxman and Canova. His 'Tinted Venus' (1851) is the best-known of his attempts to revive the Classical practice of colouring statues.

Below: Prince Albert's model lodging house, erected in Hyde Park for the Great Exhibition, was one of many high-minded attempts to ameliorate the problem of housing the poor.

Right: The elaborately carved handles and over-large cartouches of this Minton Neo-Rococo potpourri point to its nineteenth-century manufacture.

Below and below right: The monument to the Duke of Wellington by Alfred Stevens (1818–75) in London's St Paul's Cathedral. The victor of Waterloo is depicted in heroic equestrian pose atop a marble architectural conceit of sombre Classicism, flanked by allegorical figures of Valour and Cowardice.

when he produced the winning entry in a competition to design the memorial to the Duke of Wellington for St Paul's Cathedral in 1856. The shrine was inspired by Matteo Camero's early sixteenth-century high altar in the church of St John and St Paul in Venice. At St Paul's in 1864 he also executed some beautiful mosaics which ornament the spandrel panels between the main arches. They depict three Old Testament figures: Isaiah, Jeremiah and Daniel. These mosaics echo the style of fresco work in the Sistine Chapel, and Stevens was often regarded as a 'mere copyist of Michelangelo'.

SYKES AND SEMPER
Stevens' influence as a teacher inspired by the

glories of the Italian Renaissance, can be seen in many of the projects of the 1860s and 1870s by his pupils from the School of Design. The most prominent of these was Godfrey Sykes, a key figure behind the decoration of the Victoria and Albert Museum. Here Sykes designed the ceramic and terracotta ornamentation that characterises the western wing of the building. He also designed a subsequently influential alphabet in earthenware tiles for the refreshment room in the museum, which revived a sixteenth-century Venetian tradition of letters decorated with figures symbolising each initial.

Another member of the Cole Group was the German emigré Gottfried Semper. With his encyclopedic knowledge of the history of architecture and ornamental style, Semper was a key supporter of the Renaissance Revival.

HIGH VICTORIAN GOTHIC

The mid-Victorian period saw the culmination of the Gothic Revival which had been progressing in a rather sporadic fashion since the 1750s. In the eighteenth century, interest in the Gothic was the dilettante hobby of aristocrats and the rich. Under the influence of romantic novels by writers like Hugh Walpole (who owned an early Gothic Revival home, Strawberry Hill) and Sir Walter Scott, men like William Beckford at Fonthill Abbey and Sir Roger Newdigate at Arbury Hall planned homes in the Gothic style. For these patrons, the style was a picturesque diversion rather than an exercise in historical veracity. Like Scott's *Waverley* novels, these buildings were to their owners places where they could escape from the realities of business and politics and dream of a chivalrous time of medieval knights and pageants.

Edward Blore published a rhapsodic book

called *Monumental Ruins* in 1826 which became an important source book for early nineteenth century designers and patrons fantasising about a picturesque past. At Goodrich House in Herefordshire, Sir Samuel Rush Meyrick employed Blore to create a 'Hastilude Chamber' in which to house his famous collection of armour.

Related to the rise of the Gothic was the increasing popularity of antiquaria. Led by academic and literary taste in the late eighteenth century, in the early part of the nineteenth century it became highly fashionable to collect and decorate one's home with antiques and authentic architectural details. The Gothic encouraged the taste for medievalist objects: suits of armour, heraldic motifs, stained glass and carved masonry.

Many writers have characterised this phase of interest in the Gothic as merely a pastiche when compared with the mid-Victorian highly moral and clerical attitude to it. But it must be noted that this romantic and picturesque phase of the Gothic was underpinned by some serious scholarship, such as E J Wilson's *Specimens of Gothic Architecture* of 1821 to 1823.

Overleaf left: The late-medieval-style drawing room of Eastnor Castle, Herefordshire, 1840.

Overleaf right: One of the reading rooms in the library of the House of Lords designed by Augustus Pugin. Converted to Catholicism in 1835, Pugin believed that a medieval-Gothic revival would encourage a return to pre-Reformation spiritual values.

Above: Wallpaper designed by Augustus Pugin for the Houses of Parliament. Incorporating the Tudor Rose and the portcullis intertwined with the royal cipher, it was produced by S Scott, J G Crace.

Opposite: Pugin's work can be admired in the House of Lords' library (below left) and, more particularly , in the lords' chamber itself. Here the magnificent painted and gilded throne canopy (below right) bears the royal coat of arms (top right) surmounted by effigies of St George and four knights (top left).

A W N Pugin

The Gothic Revival shifted into a new phase of intensity under the influence of a young designer and, more significantly, theoretician: August Welby Northmore Pugin. In the year of his death, 1851, he wrote: 'My writings, much more than what I have been able to do, have revolutionised the taste of England'.

A prolific designer of furnishings, stained glass, ceramics and metalwork, Pugin's most important designs were for the furniture and fittings for the Houses of Parliament under the architect Charles Barry. This commission, secured by Barry in 1835, was a major milestone in the story of the Gothic Revival in the nineteenth century, parliament having decided that it was the appropriate style for this most important of national buildings.

Despite achieving his place in the history of art for these designs, Pugin regarded himself as first and foremost an architect, although he received only a small number of commissions, including Scarisbrick Hall. His historical significance, however, lies in his activities as a propagandist for the Gothic style.

The Pre-Raphaelite influence

The influence of the Gothic was not restricted to architecture and the applied arts. Through the inspired pen of John Ruskin, the Middle Ages called the most radical of mid-Victorian artists to take up their brushes and crusade both morally and aesthetically.

The Pre-Raphaelite Brotherhood was the outcome of discussions between William Holman Hunt, Dante Gabriel Rossetti and John Everett Millais in 1848. This trio of English painters decided to challenge the entrenched art establishment of the day and revitalise English art. Gathering together a number of other artists, a brotherhood of seven was

formed. In choosing the name 'Pre-Raphaelite', they demonstrated their dislike of much art after the time of Raphael.

Although they saw themselves as artistic revolutionaries, the subjects of their paintings were the classic themes of romantic art through the ages. Their period of ascendancy was during the 1850s, but even by the middle of that decade the Pre-Raphaelite Brotherhood had begun to dissolve.

WILLIAM MORRIS

The Pre-Raphaelite torch was held aloft by a number of young Victorian designers, among whom the most prominent were William Morris and Edward Burne-Jones. Fired both by the Gothic Revival and the example of the Pre-Raphaelites, Morris and his associates developed a language of decorative art that left behind the blind historicism of their predecessors and pointed toward later design in the twentieth century.

'The Firm', as Morris, Marshall, Faulkner and Company was known, was formed in 1861. Although the Victorian design establishment was highly critical of these amateurs, it was not untroubled by their arrival on the scene because they had the support of the leading critic and design thinker of the day, John Ruskin. Despite the obvious distance between the Cole Group and Morris and his colleagues, echoes of the former can be heard in Morris' calls for 'artists of repute' to devote their energies to the decorative arts.

Initially, they were only able to secure commissions for stained glass, notably at All

Right: The Pre-Raphaelite painter William Holman Hunt's The Light of the World *achieved the status of a Protestant icon.*

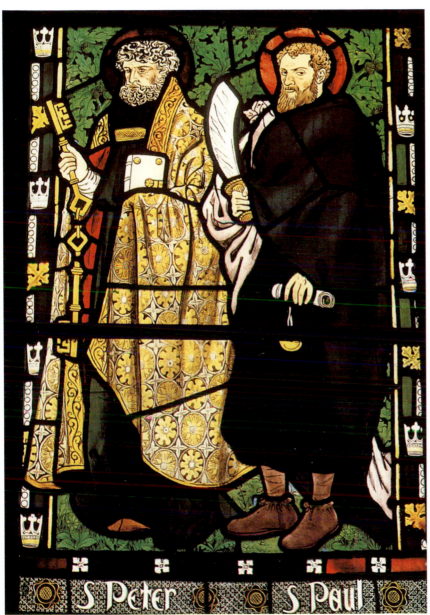

S Peter   S Paul

Saints' church in Bingley in 1864, designed by Richard Norman Shaw. By the end of the 1860s Morris & Co had become fashionable in artistic circles. The company's designs in that decade were delightfully simple, usually drawing their inspiration from nature. In Morris' wallpapers and fabrics, like 'Daisy' and 'Fruit' (both produced during the 1860s), floral motifs were highly stylised and flattened, in subdued, tasteful colours.

Left: Madox Brown and Morris designed this stained-glass window for Middleton Cheney , Northamptonshire, in 1865.

Below: Burne-Jones' window for Christ Church Cathedral, Oxford, 1871.

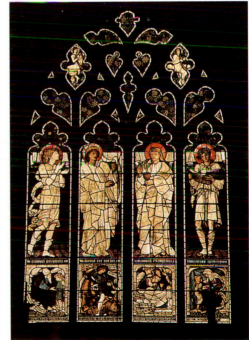

But underneath these beautiful designs for fabrics, wallpapers, stained glass, ceramics and furniture lay a very considered philosophy about the alienation wrought by Victorian industry and the democratic potential in art. Following Ruskin, Morris established the link between industrialisation and the decline in the standards of design in manufacturing. Through its products, the members of the company sought to redirect the society in which they lived.

Morris defined handicraft as 'the expression of man of his pleasure in labour', and this philosophy moved him to learn all the craft techniques in which he designed. He declared his aim to make 'artists craftsmen and craftsmen artists'. The irony of Morris' socialist aspirations and his desire to bring his own aesthetic within reach of the common man, however, was that inevitably the price of his handcrafted designs was in almost all cases well beyond the means of the Victorian working classes.

THE QUEEN ANNE REVIVAL STYLE

The Queen Anne Revival of the 1870s was led by architects, but its influence can be seen in other areas of art and design. It was a bridge from the High Victorian period to the final decades of the century, when architects and designers shed historicism and developed genuinely new stylistic languages.

Queen Anne interiors drew upon an eclectic range of styles. Fashionable artistic taste dictated that subtle, natural colours were preferable to modern ones, such as mauve and magenta. Antiques were also in vogue and eighteenth-century Chelsea and Worcester porcelain and Chippendale furniture were considered highly fashionable. The influence of the East could often be found in Persian carpets and Japanese fans and plates. This eclecticism resulted in many cluttered and crowded rooms filled to the ceiling with bric–à-brac. In this respect, owners of Queen Anne-style homes chose to depart from the self-consciously humble origins of this style.

EASTERN INFLUENCES

In the nineteenth century the West encountered the East through colonial life, wars, commercial expansion, travel, popular journalism and scholarly works. Writers and artists such as Rudyard Kipling romanticised the East.

Although Western collectors had been acquiring the triumph of Eastern craftsmanship for many centuries, the East was brought to life for a broader public through international exhibitions. The Chinese section at the Great Exhibition of 1851 and the Japanese Court at the London International Exhibition of 1862 were both critical and popular successes. This exhibition triggered a fashion for all things Japanese and the firm of Liberty, founded in 1875 by Arthur Liberty, was the consequence of his enthusiasm for these exhibits.

E W GODWIN

Architects and designers led fashionable taste by incorporating Japanese characteristics into their work. The key figure in this development was Edward William Godwin, who began his career strongly under the influence of John Ruskin's ideas about the Gothic in the 1850s and who is believed to have designed the first item of Japanese-style furniture in England in 1867. In fact, his knowledge of Japanese craftsmanship was very thin, and he derived the style of his furniture designs from details in *Hokusai* prints.

In 1877 he designed a house in Chelsea for

Opposite page: Wiliam Morris' 'Larkspur' design was produced as both a wallpaper and a printed cotton.

Left and far left: In 1881, two years after Morris had set himself up at Merton Abbey, he patented 17 printed-cotton designs, including 'Wey' (far left) and the still popular 'Strawberry thief'. 'Medway' (left) was designed and registered in 1885.

the American painter James Whistler which was the fullest expression of the Japanese influence up until that time. Its interiors were very simple, with white walls, matting covering the floor, plain curtains and each room full of Chinese porcelain and Japanese prints.

THE ARTS AND CRAFTS MOVEMENT
William Morris' thought and practice were the primary inspiration behind the avant-garde of the 1880s: the Arts and Crafts Movement. This loose alliance of artists, craftsmen and designers united around a twin aesthetic and social philosophy, based on the importance of making.

THE CENTURY GUILD
The movement gathered momentum with the formation of the Century Guild in 1882 by Arthur Heygate Mackmurdo and Selwyn Image. Mackmurdo had travelled through Italy

in 1874 with Ruskin as his companion and had absorbed much of the latter's social and aesthetic ideology. As an architect, he aimed to design, build and furnish complete buildings, down to the minutest of details: from the whole façade down to each key hole. He lamented the decline of the guild system of the Middle Ages which would have presented the corporate means with which to do this and resolved to form his own guild of like-minded people who could work together to evolve a collective style.

The Century Guild was constituted by Selwyn Image, a poet and designer; Herbert Horne, a designer of fabrics and wallpaper; Clement Heaton, who specialised in *cloisonné*-enamael work; and George Heywood Sumner, who was renowned for his *sgraffito* pottery designs. The guild aimed to turn design into art, overturning the prevailing aesthetic harmony, and to develop an

Right: Japanese imports of the 1860s had a great impact, as reflected in James Hadley's Royal Worcester porcelain vases (1872).

Below: Pieces like this copy of a sixteenth-century Persian bottle were displayed by Minton at the London International Exhibition of 1871.

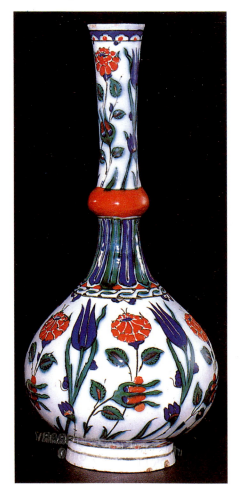

aesthetic that was appropriate to its own time. Its members rejected the historicism of Victorian art and architecture in favour of an artistic language derived from nature, as exemplified in Mackmurdo's title page for his *Wren's City Churches* (1883), remarkable for its use of undulating and whiplashing floral motifs which prefigured Art Nouveau.

THE ART WORKERS GUILD

The conscientious core of the Arts and Crafts Movement was found in the Art Workers Guild, founded in 1884, which was later absorbed into the Arts and Crafts Exhibition Society of 1888. The guild included some of the leading designers of the day, including Lewis F Day, W R Lethaby, John D Sedding and Walter Crane. They held similar ambitions to Morris and their colleagues in Mackmurdo's Century Guild, aiming to revive the decorative arts by improving standards of design and craftsmanship. With the formation of the Arts and Crafts Exhibition Society they sought to challenge the Victorian art and design establishments of the Royal Academy and the Royal Institute of British Architects.

A series of exhibitions was held in the late 1880s and 1890s. Sharing Morris' belief in the indivisible unity of the arts, they aimed to show fine art alongside decorative objects, so that paintings by Walter Crane could be found hanging alongside an elegant brass teapot designed by C F A Voysey.

THE GUILD OF HANDICRAFT

C R Ashbee's Guild of Handicraft, founded in 1888, was the last of the Arts and Crafts guilds of the nineteenth century and, appropriately, it held the most complete vision of Arts and Crafts life. Ashbee developed his ideas as a teacher of Ruskinian philosophy in a working-men's college in Whitechapel in the 1880s. He devised the idea of a pedagogical guild in which young men would be taught to design in a number of fields. Their designs would then be produced in workshops by craftsmen and sold to the public; the revenue from these sales, he envisaged, would finance the organisation.

In 1902, after 12 years based in London's East End, Ashbee moved the guild, the guildsmen and their families to Chipping Camden, in Gloucestershire. Here 150 men, women and children established a life based on the values of hard work and communal living. But the scheme failed under the economic pressure to sell their furniture, ceramics and metalware to a late-Victorian market that was not satisfied with such well-made works of simple beauty.

INTERNATIONAL INFLUENCE

The guild achieved greater fame on the European continent, however. In 1897, for example, the Grand Duke of Hesse commissioned designs from C R Ashbee and Baillie Scott which were made by the Guild of Handicrafts. Influenced by their Arts and Crafts philosophy, the duke formed his own artists' colony in Darmstadt along the lines of the Guild of Handicrafts. Another group of artists and designers influenced by the philosophy of the Arts and Crafts Movement was the Wiener Werkstätte, formed by Joseph Hoffmann and Koloman Moser in 1903. Morris and Ruskin's influence was also to be found in America, where figures like Frank Lloyd Wright took Arts and Crafts' themes and fixations and developed a visionary design practice that can be said to have anticipated Modernist design of the twentieth century.

ART NOUVEAU

The Arts and Crafts Movement was also a major inspiration behind Art Nouveau, the leading movement in art and design in the late 1890s and early years of the twentieth century in continental Europe. Stylistic precedents for Art Nouveau can be found in British design of the 1880s, for example, in the Gothic architect William Burges' own house, built in Kensington between 1875 and 1880, and in A H Mackmurdo's works. But, more importantly, the Arts and Crafts Movement raised the status of applied art from that of a commercial trade to an art form, though in England Art Nouveau was widely dismissed by

Below: The geometrical shape of this elegant walnut cabinet by E W Godwin, embellished with carved Japanese boxwood plaques and ivory monkey handles, displays a distinct Japanese influence.

practitioners because it lacked the critical social philosophy that was so crucial to the Arts and Crafts Movement.

Very few British artists and designers came close to the Art Nouveau spirit found on the continent. The few that did – the Scottish designer Charles Rennie Mackintosh, for instance – were even more antithetical to the Victorian age than their sober Arts and Crafts colleagues, who at least preached the values of hard work and national form.

THE LEGACY OF VICTORIAN STYLE

Despite the somewhat clouded picture we have of trends in art and design in the late nineteenth century, partly because of the character of its leading practitioners – Morris, Ashbee, Mackmurdo and others – the dominating concern was to find solutions to the problem of Victorian style. In turning away from historicism and conspicuous excess, these artists and designers pointed towards the new trends of the twentieth century.

Furthermore, these late-nineteenth-century movements were concerned with larger issues than just style. They issued a challenge to Victorian society and its dearly held values. For Ashbee and the Guild of Handicraft, this entailed a considered retreat into communal living, and for others, such as Aubrey Beardsley, it took the less reasoned form of displays of decadence designed to shock middle-class morals.

To Queen Victoria and her husband Prince Albert, Victorian style, as found in the best British works at the Great Exhibition of 1851, confirmed the success of their age. At the end of the century, Victoria's grandson, Ernst Ludwig, Grand Duke of Hesse, looked to the English designers Baillie Scott and Ashbee to point towards a new world. Above the entrance to his artists' colony, intended as the cornerstone of a new Utopian city, were the words: 'Let the artist show his world that which has never been nor will be'.

Above: Mackintosh's imaginative use of metalwork and stained glass, as seen in the doors to the Willow Tea Rooms, had a tremendous influence on the development of European Art Nouveau.

Far left: Design for a dado by Walter Crane.

Left: Beardsley's designs for the Yellow Book *covers introduced a new illustrative style featuring heavy black masses, evidence of Eastern influence.*

VICTORIAN ARCHITECTURE

Mid-nineteenth-century architecture and design was trapped in a paradox. The Victorians lived in an age of amazing inventiveness and imagination. They were as aware of the progress made in their time as any historian today. But while engineers, entrepreneurs and scientists were building the future, 'the mother of the arts' – architecture – appeared to be sinking into even greater retrospection, dominated as it was by historicism.

Previous page: London's Royal Albert Hall, designed by Captain Francis Fowke, was built between 1867 and 1871.

Below: Horace Walpole's Strawberry Hill, Twickenham.

Historicism was widely regarded as a problem, even by those architects whose practice was most firmly entrenched in one of the many historical styles of the day. George Gilbert Scott, the Gothicist, wrote in 1850: 'I am no mediaevalist, I do not advocate the styles of the Middle Ages as such. If we had a distinctive architecture of our own day, worthy of the greatness of the age, I should be content to follow it; but we have not'.

PROPONENTS OF GOTHIC AND CLASSICAL
The proponents of each divergent style believed that it had the most to offer modern

man. Scott chose the Gothic because he believed that it combined the spiritual in its 'Christian' forms and the rational in that it provided building solutions for every kind of architectural problem, from his monumental St Pancras railway station to the humblest of cottages. Conversely, the Classicists – men like Sir Robert Smirke, the architect of the British Museum – believed that their chosen architectural language embodied the great timeless, transcending values of art, democracy and civilisation. Smirke and Scott shared a common reverence for times past.

SUBDIVIDING STYLES
Furthermore, beyond the very general architectural classifications of Classical and Gothic, a series of subdivisions can be drawn up, whose proponents were pitched against each other. Until the Enlightenment of the eighteenth century, architecture had followed a set of conventions that established a hierarchy of appropriate forms. The monumental Doric order, for example, was considered suitable for buildings such as prisons, whereas the more decorative Corinthian was used in buildings such as clubs. With the rise of notions of the

picturesque in the late eighteenth century, these Classical rules of design broke down. Architects began to search for novelty and variety. Great architecture came to be seen less as the successful application of established rules and more as a source of delight.

STRAWBERRY HILL
The earliest Gothic Revival buildings of the mid-eighteenth century paid little heed to historical accuracy. They were the projects of romantics and enthusiasts rather than pedants. Horace Walpole's home, Strawberry Hill,

Left: Coe & Hofland's design for the new Foreign Office building, to be located near Downing Street, was one of many submitted in the Classical style.

Below: The Houses of Parliament, designed by architect Charles Barry, and the famous clock tower, Big Ben (detail).

begun in 1749, originally contained a number of Classical elements, such as a Palladian chimney piece in the style of William Kent. He augmented these details with a diverse range of Gothic forms: the staircase wallpaper was derived from ornamentation found in Worcester Cathedral; St Alban's Abbey provided the inspiration for the doors to the gallery; and Richard Bentley designed a set of chairs to match some sixteenth-century stained glass that Walpole had installed there.

CATEGORISING SUBSTYLES

During the nineteenth century British architects began to be concerned with greater veracity and historical styles were divided into periods and substyles. Thomas Rickman's book *Attempt to Discriminate the Styles in English Architecture* of 1819 established the three categories still used to describe the Gothic today: Early English, Decorated and Perpendicular. By the middle years of the nineteenth century, each of these styles had its

supporters. As an example, although most Victorian Gothic buildings were typically in the Perpendicular style, the great architectural theorist August Welby Northmore Pugin was a dedicated proponent of the Decorated (preferring to call it 'English Middle Pointed').

Similarly, Classical architecture was subdivided into a number of styles: Neo-Classical or Palladian and so on. The architect and archaeologist Charles Cockerill, in his support for a variant called 'Classical Antiquity', was just as concerned with historical veracity as his Gothic counterparts.

ARCHITECTURE IN CRISIS

Victorian architectural practice hit a crisis in the middle of the century because of this highly self-conscious and academic approach to historical style. Victorian thinking was widely based on a belief in the evolutionary nature of progress, but in their new-found concern with accurately recreating the achievements of the past architects hit a dead end. Scott acknowledged this, writing: 'The peculiar characteristics of the present day, as compared with all former periods, is this – that we are acquainted with the history of art'.

The crisis in Victorian architecture, and in particular its fixation with historical styles, is neatly encapsulated in the story of the competition for the Foreign Office building in Whitehall in 1856. This episode not only reveals the extent to which architects were bound by historicism, but also the meaning

Above: Now a museum, Monkwearmouth Station was opened in 1848. Local architect Thomas Moore was responsible for the Classical design. The building's frontage employs a pediment supported by columns of the Ionic order.

Above: The chromolithographed frontispiece to Pugin's Glossary of Ecclesiastical Ornament and Costume, Compiled and Illustrated from Ancient Authorities and Examples *(1844), one of several major works of research on medieval Gothic styles.*

Right: This coloured engraving of 1837 shows the London terminus of the London and Birmingham Railway at Euston Square.

that was attached to particular styles within Victorian society.

THE FOREIGN OFFICE COMPETITION

By the mid-1850s the Foreign Office had outgrown its headquarters. Lord Palmerston's Liberal government announced a competition to build new offices on a site near Downing Street. Most of the projects submitted were in the Classical style and the winning design by H B Garling was heavily influenced by the new Louvre building in Paris. Palmerston did not like this design, and set Sir James Pennethorne, architect to the Board of Works, the task of designing the building.

George Gilbert Scott was one of the small number of Gothic architects who had submitted a design in the original competition and had been awarded third place. On hearing that the winning design was to be rejected and a non-competitor commissioned, Scott lobbied strongly to have his project reconsidered.

There were many in parliament who supported Scott, for it was felt that the Gothic was the most appropriate architectural style for a major state commission. This architectural language was argued by its proponents to be a singularly national style, echoing the nearby Westminster Hall, the Henry VII Chapel of Westminster Abbey and the still incomplete

new Houses of Parliament by Charles Barry. The Gothic style, particularly in its Perpendicular form, was also associated with the Anglican religion and nationalist and royalist politics.

In 1858 a new Tory government came into power, bringing a number of Scott's supporters in with it. One, Lord John Manners, was made First Commissioner of Works and appointed Scott as architect to the scheme. However, another political swing occurred and in 1859 the Liberal Party was brought back into power. When Palmerston suggested that another architect might be able to meet his demands, Scott capitulated and produced further designs in a 'Byzantine' style – none met the prime minister's approval. Scott was only able to secure Palmerston's necessary consent by compromising with an Italian Renaissance-style design.

The conflict between Scott and Palmerston had little to do with the fitness of the design: it came about because of their divergent stylistic preferences. When the building was complete, it differed little from Scott's original design. The building, in Portland stone and coloured granite, is dominated by an Italianate tower that could just have easily have been erected in polychromatic bands of brick and carved masonry underneath a tower mimicking the Venetian early Renaissance.

CLASSICAL ARCHITECTURE
Although other architectural styles, such as the Gothic, had more vigorous advocates and were winning many of the prestigious competitions, 'the Greek' continued to be popular in certain fields of design, such as municipal building and memorial sculpture.

Although Sir Robert Smirke's British Museum, the most prominent Victorian Neo-Classical building in London, was completed in 1847, it was designed in the 1820s and so really belongs to an earlier period of architectural taste.

In Scotland and the industrial cities of the north of England the Neo-Classical style continued to be popular; perhaps the greatest of these buildings is J A Hansom's Birmingham Town Hall, opened in 1849. In Scotland, a number of late-Classical buildings were erected in the 1850s, including W H Playfair's

Below: The chamber of the House of Lords designed by Augustus Pugin, who was responsible for the interior and exterior decoration of the Houses of Parliament in medieval Gothic style.

Below: The central hall of the Natural History Museum, London. The inclusion of medieval Italianate features reflects the celebrated critic John Ruskin's broader approach to Gothic Revivalism.

National Gallery of Scotland in Edinburgh of 1850–54 and Alexander Thomson's Caledonia Road Free Church in Glasgow of 1856–57. Furthermore, railway companies continued to commission Neo-Classical buildings in the 1840s and 1850s.

PUGIN AND THE POPULARISATION OF THE GOTHIC STYLE

As a keen student of architectural history, Pugin brought to the Gothic Revival a moral and ideological urgency which his predecessors had lacked. Through his books – and, to a lesser

degree, his designs – he harangued Victorian Britain on the themes of spirituality and honesty. He saw in the Middle Ages a sense of social order and Christian values that were lacking in his own era. Victorian architecture must therefore also be deficient, he argued.

Pugin developed a philosophy of architecture which centred around the model of English Gothic of the fourteenth century. For Pugin, it was firstly the national architecture and, as such, correct for Victorian Britain; secondly, it was a Christian architecture in its concern with 'upwards', in contrast to variants of Classicism which were symbolic of Mammon; and, thirdly, it was an architecture fit for the purposes to which it was put.

This philosophy was augmented with ideas about honesty in architecture. Pugin believed that historical details should not be copied unless they had a useful function. For example, he rejected castellated forms and battlements as inappropriate in the Victorian world. But conversely, to prove that the Gothic was a flexible and evolving architectural language, he set about designing two railway bridges – highly charged symbols of the industrial age.

Pugin stated that 'There should be no features about a building which are not necessary for convenience, construction or propriety'. Ornamentation was to be avoided unless it 'enriched the essential construction of the building'. This was not an out-and-out rejection of ornamentation in architecture but a concern with 'propriety'. In Pugin's thought,

a clear architectural hierarchy existed which equated decoration with decorum. He felt that it was entirely suitable for the area around an altar to be treated with the richest ornamental detail but that areas like naves should be left plain. Pugin's concern with truth meant that these functional parts of buildings were not to be disguised but to be revealed honestly.

JOHN RUSKIN

Pugin's influence on his contemporaries was muted by his Roman Catholicism, which restricted his contact with other influential promoters of the Gothic. John Ruskin was another major theorist of the style who distanced himself from Pugin because of his religion, although many of Pugin's ideas

Left: The soaring metal beams and struts of Brighton Station's train shed's roof, installed in 1882 by H E Wallis, attempt to imitate the vertical thrust of Victorian Gothic.

surface in Ruskin's key writings: *The Seven Lamps of Architecture* (1849) and *The Stones of Venice* (1851–53). In these texts we find the same concerns with craftsmanship, honesty, Godliness and national style, although with different emphases. Ruskin's main lines of attack were against what he called 'dishonest' and machine-made ornamentation. Ruskin also travelled widely through Europe in the 1840s and was greatly influenced by Italian medieval art and architecture.

Accordingly, Ruskin was highly critical of the Crystal Palace and its contents and the design theories of the Cole Group. He believed that the best example for young British designers could be found in the craft traditions established in the Middle Ages. Like Pugin, he found here a model of a happy society which produced beautiful things and concluded that these two facts were not unrelated.

HIGH VICTORIAN GOTHIC

In true Victorian fashion, and under Ruskin's influence, architects began to include French, German and Italian Gothic elements in their buildings. In addition to a larger variety of styles, the proponents of the High Victorian Gothic advocated a wider range of materials than their predecessors, including marble and coloured brick.

The University Museum, Oxford (1855–60), was the realisation of a number of Ruskinian ideals. The building also marked the end of the dominance of the English Perpendicular

Opposite page: The ceiling of St Paul's Cathedral, London, designed by Sir William Richmond (1892–92).

Right: The Royal Courts of Justice in London's Strand were begun by G E Street in 1874.

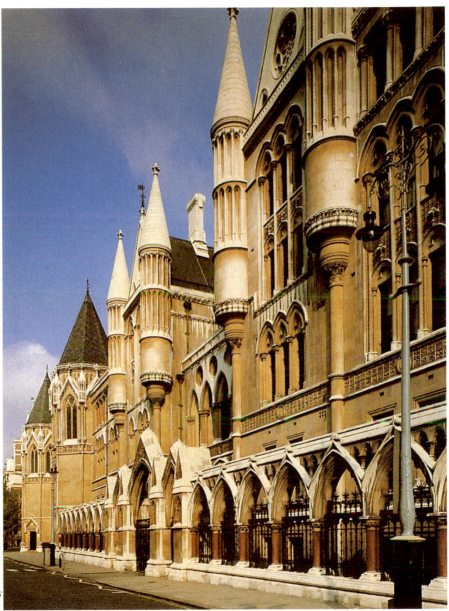

style used to such strong effect by Barry and Pugin in the new Houses of Parliament, and the beginning of the High Gothic Revival. Through Ruskin's influence two supporters of the High Victorian Gothic style, Thomas Deane and Benjamin Woodward, were commissioned to design the museum. This beautiful building displays a broad range of architectural devices: constructional poly-chromy borrowed from Venetian Gothic of the fourteenth century; a sharp roof topped with a metal finial that echoes Flemish Gothic; and attendant buildings, housing laboratories, inspired by the fourteenth-century Abbot's Kitchen at Glastonbury Abbey. Here the thrusting verticality of the 'English Pointed' style gave way to an Italian horizontality and the heart of the museum was a tiled courtyard under a canopy of glass and Gothic ironwork.

THE ECCLESIOLOGICAL SOCIETY

The Gothic was strongly identified as an Anglican style. The Cambridge Camden Society, for example, was established in 1836 to promote Anglicanism and the Gothic archi-tecture of the fourteenth century. This group, renamed the Ecclesiological Society in 1846, exerted an influence on such projects as Anthony Salvin's restoration of the Holy Sepulchre Church in Cambridge and Sydney Smirke's improvements to the Temple Church in London in the early 1840s. The society also produced a book entitled *Instrumenta Ecclesiastica*, which was a kind of pattern book for church fittings and decorations. It also

Right: The central hall of G E Street's Royal Courts of Justice gives access to the various courts and is 238 feet (72.5m) long and 80 feet (24.4m) high.

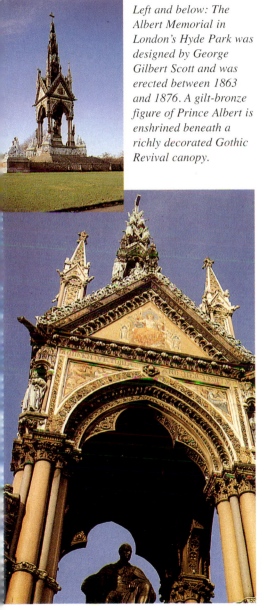

Left and below: The Albert Memorial in London's Hyde Park was designed by George Gilbert Scott and was erected between 1863 and 1876. A gilt-bronze figure of Prince Albert is enshrined beneath a richly decorated Gothic Revival canopy.

employed such well-known Gothic architects as William Butterfield.

WILLIAM BUTTERFIELD

Butterfield was a key architect in the development of High Victorian Gothic. His first major building project was All Saints' church in London, commissioned by the Ecclesiological Society in 1849. Butterfield had been strongly under the influence of Pugin's ideas, but this scheme marked a new stage in his thought. Built on a restricted site in Westminster, the church was reported to have had the tallest spire in London at that date. It was simply decorated with bands of coloured brick. In the higher parts of the spire, and in the clergy residence, this simple ornamental effect was further enhanced by diagonal patterning.

GEORGE EDMUND STREET

George Edmund Street followed Butterfield's example at All Saints' in using brick polychromy in many of his buildings. This decorative device, intended to reveal the structural simplicity of Gothic architecture, became a characteristic aspect of High Victorian Gothic design. In his books, such as *Brick and Marble in the Middle Ages* (1855), Street helped to stimulate the taste for rich, banded brickwork in architecture. In such buildings as St James the Less (1859–61) and St Mary Magdalene (1867–78) in London, Street was able to realise

Below: The imposing frontage of George Gilbert Scott's St Pancras Station (1867–74) incorporates elements from French and Italian Gothic architecture.

Below: The clock tower of St Pancras Station, designed by George Gilbert Scott, reaches a height of 300 feet (91.4m).

his talents as an artist in brick.

As a Gothicist, Street did not restrict his architectural practice to churches, and he designed a number of secular buildings in this style. In fact, the last major state commission to be built in the Gothic style was Street's Royal Courts of Justice, on the Strand in London, which he secured in a competition in 1866. The building was begun in 1874 and was completed eight years later. Its façade is a complicated, asymmetrical series of turrets, castellated details and irregularly placed, arched windows, fronting a great hall with a high, vaulted ceiling.

GEORGE GILBERT SCOTT
George Gilbert Scott was another prominent architect who employed the Gothic as a secular style. After his Albert Memorial, he is most famous for the Midland Hotel at St Pancras railway station in London, designed in 1865. The hotel is a marvellous, curved building, climaxing in a clock tower and a spire at its western end. But beyond its picturesque qualities, in this building Scott also sought to prove that the Gothic was a suitable building style for the modern world, and in it cantilevered iron girders arched over open spaces.

THE QUEEN ANNE REVIVAL
The 'Queen Anne Movement' was a label attached to a small group of artists and designers in the 1870s that stuck. It was a misnomer on two accounts: it had little to do with Queen Anne or the early years of the eighteenth century, nor did it constitute a 'movement', for those associated with it lacked the self-consciousness of a cabal like the Pre-Raphaelite Brotherhood or the intellectual programme of the Arts and Crafts Movement of the 1880s.

The Gothic started to lose its exclusively Christian associations in the late 1850s and 1860s. As practised by younger Gothicists – Burne-Jones, Rossetti and Burges – it became a highly aetheticised style. Younger architects and designers following in the wake of these figures, including Philip Webb and Richard Norman Shaw, were to form the nucleus. Both had worked in George Edmund Street's architectural practice in the 1850s and began to reject the out-and-out medievalism of the Gothic Revival; others felt that the style had been corrupted by commerce. They came under the sway of intellectuals like Walter Pater, who argued that 'all periods, types, schools of taste, are in themselves equal'. After years of studying French thirteenth-century cathedrals and fourteenth-century Venice, young architects now felt themselves at liberty to look at English domestic and vernacular traditions, such as tile-hanging, weather-boarding and half-timbering. The embryonic Queen Anne circle developed a cult of Englishness.

But true to Pater's thesis, Queen Anne was an amalgamation of a broader range of influences than merely national ones. In Queen Anne architecture, for example, traces of Dutch and Japanese styles can be found. Philip Webb's later houses, built between 1879 and 1891, even display the marked influence of Classical and Elizabethan design, for example, his own house, Standen (1891–92), in Sussex.

RICHARD NORMAN SHAW
The Queen Anne style is epitomised by a number of houses built by Shaw in Chelsea in the 1870s, described by William Morris as 'elegantly fantastic'. All combine similar details composed in ingenious ways, giving each its individual character. Old Swan House

(1875–77), overlooking the Thames, has an immediate appearance of rather plain symmetry and regularity. But Shaw took great pleasure in small details, such as the positioning of different window types. The first floor has small, paned oriel windows with ornamental stonework decorated with swans; the over-sailed second floor has slender bowed and sash windows set flush with the brickwork; and high dormer windows push out of the pitched roof. The unique character of the building comes from Shaw's ability to compose in a number of English architectural traditions.

Oriel windows were prominent in Shaw's two houses in Cadogan Square in Chelsea, designed in 1877, as were other Queen Anne features: pitched roofs, red brick and ornamental stonework. But the appearance of these buildings was quite different to the Old Swan House: they took on a Flemish character, with dominant, Dutch-style gables emphasising their verticality and with their porches capped with broken pediments in the seventeenth-century fashion.

BEDFORD PARK

The peak of the Queen Anne Movement came with the building of the Bedford Park suburb on the western edges of London. Inspired by the fashionable cult of ruralism, Jonathan T Carr, a property speculator, planned to build a 'village' for the artistic middle classes and approached E W Godwin and Shaw to design the first homes in 1877. The 500 houses that they, and other architects, such as E J May and J C Dollman, built here, were modest homes in leafy streets with picturesque names like 'Queen Anne's Grove' and 'Marlborough Crescent'. The quaint Queen Anne style employed for these houses in Bedford Park can also be found in its church, school of art

Above: Architect George Gilbert Scott was not only responsible for St Pancras Station's exterior, but also for the interior of the station's hotel, whose grand staircase was supported on iron girders decorated with fine Gothic detailing.

and pub (or 'inn', as it was apt to be called). The church of St Michael and All Angels designed by Shaw, constructed in 1879, was unusual because it lacked a spire – a notably aesthetic gesture. The significance of this 'village' lay not in architectural novelty, for most of its buildings were plain, domestic forms originating in Tudor or Stuart England, but in Carr's vision of an artistic community living in a semi-rural setting.

THE INFLUENCE OF THE QUEEN ANNE STYLE

The Queen Anne Movement had a greater impact on the fabric of Britain's cities than any other revivalist architectural style of the nineteenth century. It was largely a domestic affair, and its importance lies in the thousands of suburban homes, pubs, hotels and shops built in its wake.

All the leading Queen Anne architects produced designs for such commonplace buildings. In 1876, for example, Ernest George designed a shop for the firm of Thomas Goode and Company in London's South Audley Street, in which glass and ceramics were sold. It is an elegant building in the Flemish style, with prominent gables and chimneys. Similarly, Shaw's place in the history of architecture was largely secured by his New Zealand Chambers of 1872, which were renowned for their oriel windows. But beyond these architectural heroes, innumerable practitioners across the country adopted the Queen Anne architectural language for their projects.

Although the major practitioners left the style in the 1880s and 1890s, with figures like Shaw moving closer to forms of Classicism, characteristic Queen Anne forms proved popular with thousands of home-owners.

Above: The Bedford Park housing project, described in its prospectus of 1881 as being in the 'picturesque Queen Anne style'.

Below: The Red House, Bexleyheath, Kent, was designed by Philip Webb for William Morris and was completed in 1860.

VICTORIAN FURNITURE

The seeds of a whole range of historical revivals in furniture had already germinated by the beginning of Queen Victoria's reign, chief among them being Gothic, Elizabethan, Louis XIV and Renaissance. Most were stylistically mixed, borrowing elements from one another in a way that appalled contemporary purists but delighted the public, which was not much concerned with historical accuracy.

Previous page: Elaborately carved, Neo-Rococo furniture by Henry Belter is featured in this American nineteenth-century interior.

Below: An ormulu- and gilt-decorated desk in the French style, typical of the ornate furniture amassed by wealthy Victorians.

These revivals fitted in with the needs of an increasingly affluent middle class, which, anxious to display its wealth as conspicuously as possible, made novelty a lodestar of acquisition. In furniture, the new was sought not only in design and ornamentation but also in material; exotic woods became increasingly favoured and, through the growth of a colonial empire, increasingly available. Mahogany, satinwood and rosewood continued to be favoured, as before, but even more sought after were elaborately figured (grained) woods, such as walnut and the expensive amboyna, thuja, purplewood (amaranth) and calamander (coromandel). In many instances these were combined with other types of timber, both native and imported.

Marquetry became more popular than ever, and metals were increasingly used, both as decoration – in the form of inlaid brass or ormolu (gilt-bronze) mounts – and in their own right, as cast-iron garden and other mass-produced furniture and brass bedsteads.

MANUFACTURING DEVELOPMENTS

Developments in *papier-mâché* manufacture produced a material of sufficient strength to enable it to be used not just for trays and boxes but, from the 1830s onwards, also for tables, chairs and even beds. And its decorative possibilities – it lent itself to being inlaid with pearl shell, gilded, bronzed and painted in brilliant colours on lustrous dark backgrounds – appealed to the exuberant and eclectic tastes of the Victorians.

Other manufacturing developments played a part in the growth of the florid Victorian style of decoration. One was the introduction of the coiled spring in the late 1820s, which led to the bulky upholstery with deep-buttoned seating that was characteristic of the Victorian interior. Another development was the use of spirit varnishes, known as French polish, first adopted in the Regency period and now taken up with increasing enthusiasm by furniture manufacturers, who used them to produce a brilliant 'piano finish' that far outshone the mellow lustre obtained from beeswax and turpentine. Both coiled springing and French polish were liberally applied to old, as well as new, furniture, regardless of suitability.

The introduction of wafer-thin, machine-cut veneers and

mechanically carved decoration also contributed to the extravagant Victorian style. According to the architectural and horticultural writer J C Loudon (1783–1843), all that most people of the time wanted was 'to get a display of rich workmanship at as cheap a rate as possible'.

Good-quality reproductions of French furniture continued to be made for the affluent by such firms as John Webb, Wright & Mansfield and Edwards & Roberts. At the same time, almost all manufacturers purveyed furniture in the quintessentially English styles of Chippendale, Hepplewhite and, by the end of the century, Sheraton.

TYPICAL VICTORIAN PIECES OF FURNITURE
A classic item of Victorian furniture was the *etagerê*, sometimes known as the 'whatnot'. These pieces were screens or stands supporting shelves on which were placed artistic bric-à-brac. At their most ornate, these highly decorative pieces would contain mirrors and all kinds of artistic motifs.

Another item of furniture commonly associated with the Victorian age is the davenport (although it should be noted that this piece of furniture originated in the eighteenth century, when Captain Davenport charged the firm of Gillow with producing a small, neat desk). In the late nineteenth century it had increased in popularity to the extent that it was a characteristic feature of most middle-class homes. For the affluent, these items of furniture could display the heights of Victorian cabinetmaking, with ingeniously hidden drawers, skilful marquetry and curving cabinet lids on runners, but even the more commonplace desks made by the 'furniture factories' were highly sought after, their status lying in their decorative rather than their functional aspects.

GENDER-SPECIFIC FURNITURE
Some items of Victorian furniture can be divided by gender, for the marked differences in lifestyle and dress of men and women dictated suitable furniture for each. The 'Spanish chair', for example, was designed so that women, dressed in bulky crinolines, would be able to sit and stand gracefully. It was a kind of low, armless seat which allowed these large skirts to hang gracefully over the sides of the chair. The 'grandfather', or 'firesider', were affectionate terms for the comfortable, wing-backed, upholstered armchair in which many Victorian patriarchs would relax by the hearthside.

THE AMERICAN INFLUENCE
America made a special contribution to Victorian life with the popularisation of the rocking chair. It appears to have originated

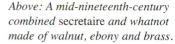

Above: A mid-nineteenth-century combined secretaire *and whatnot made of walnut, ebony and brass.*

Left: A papier-mâché *nest of tables, c. 1850. These tables have painted and gilded tops and inlays of mother-of-pearl. The largest has a painted farmyard scene after J F Herring.*

Above: A mahogany bookcase, c. *1840. The foliate decoration and 'jewels' on the pilasters of the heavy, twist-turned columns, the pierced strapwork and 'jewelled' lower doors are typically hybrid on this Elizabethan Revival bookcase.*

in both England and the American colonies in the 1760s but the classic form of rocker is known as the 'Boston'. This simple piece of furniture, found on every porch across America, evolved from the Windsor chair, with a tall, comb back and curved seat. Many people decorated their chairs with floral motifs in the style of Lambert Hitchcock, a Connecticut craftsman of the 1820s. They were imported into Britain in vast numbers and were sold as 'American Common Sense Chairs' and aids to digestion.

A number of European furniture-makers sought to surpass the simple excellence of the American rocker by producing upholstered chairs with spring rockers or tensioned-steel frames, but only Michael Thornet, an Austrian, came close with his elegant, bentwood chair exhibited at the Great Exhibition of 1851.

THE ELIZABETHAN REVIVAL

Mechanical carving was well suited to the production of furniture in the Elizabethan taste, with its panels of open decoration and strapwork (interlacing bands) and profusion of knobs and bosses. This was a style associated in the minds of the early Victorians with the 'Merrie England' and 'Olden Time' romanticised in Sir Walter Scott's novels.

Although some of its proponents, such as the architect Anthony Salvin, were serious antiquarians who paid meticulous attention to stylistic accuracy, most producers of Elizabethan Revival furniture mixed genuine Tudor motifs with the barley-sugar turnings, carved crestings (ornamentation crowning a chair) and other decorations typical of a century later.

The strictly classical architect C R Cockerell went so far as to criticise Elizabethan Revival as 'an imperfect and incongruous imitation of both Grecian and Gothic styles', but its popularity was bolstered by such publications as T F Hunt's *Exemplars of Tudor Architecture Adapted to Modern Habitations* (1830), Henry Shaw's *Specimens of Ancient Furniture* (1836) and Joseph Nash's *Mansions of England in the Olden Time* (1838–49) and it persisted well into the 1840s.

THE LOUIS XIV REVIVAL

'Louis XIV' or 'Louis Quatorze' was the label given to the vast array of furniture of more or less French influence that filled the homes of the Victorian middle classes. It actually embraced the Louis XV (Louis Quinze), or Neo-Rococo, style as well, and consequently this type of furniture is often simply referred to as 'Louis'.

In the more expensive examples, weighty Baroque forms were overlaid with asymmetrically curvaceous Rococo ornamentation and gilding was often used. But even the relatively unostentatious pieces rarely escaped Rococo flourishes, such as cabriole legs and 'C'-scrolled borders. Literal copies of French eighteenth-century marquetry pieces by the finest English craftsmen in this genre were particularly sumptuous.

Closely related to the Neo-Rococo was the naturalistic style, which looked back to the early eighteenth-century genre of the *pittoresque*, characterised by a lavish use of plant and animal forms in its decorative motifs.

Right: The carved ornamentation of this mirrored wood and marble sideboard is a heady mixture of Baroque masks, Elizabethan 'jewels', Rococo birds and culicues and Classical borders and pilasters.

THE RENAISSANCE REVIVAL

During the 1840s, Classical forms re-emerged in a revived Renaissance, or Italian, style. This was another ragbag of ornamental ideas, as shown by a contemporary writer's pronouncement that Renaissance design 'may contain the Classical orders and ornaments combined with conventional Byzantine scroll-work, Moorish tracery and interlacings, scrolled shields, fiddle-shapes and strapwork, natural imitations of animal or vegetable forms of every description and the grotesque arabesques'.

THE GOTHIC REVIVAL

The Elizabethan style and Gothic had much in common. Both were seen as particularly English and therefore patriotic; both were rooted in the cult of the picturesque; both were adopted by romantics hungry for novelty; and both primarily used native woods, such as oak or walnut.

PUGIN

Gothic architectural embellishments, such as crockets, cusps and pinnacles, were used in Victorian furniture of standard manufacture,

Right: A side cabinet made of ebony, purpleheart, ormolu, lapis lazuli and watercolour, made by Jackson of London, c. 1855. This exhibition-quality piece, in the French style of Eugène Prignot, is of the type favoured by the conspicuously rich.

but the revival of the Gothic style pursued by the English architect and interior designer A W N Pugin was much more radical. It was a search for historical accuracy and aesthetic purity and in this respect had more in common with Neo-Classicism than with the old romantic associations of the Gothic.

In 1835 Pugin published *Gothic Furniture in the Style of the 15th Century,* in which his assimilation of medieval forms of construction is evident. However, it was in the solidly simple furniture, its decoration pared to an elegant minimum, that he designed for the House of Lords and for country houses during the 1840s that Pugin most nearly attained his interior-design ideals. These pieces clearly exerted a

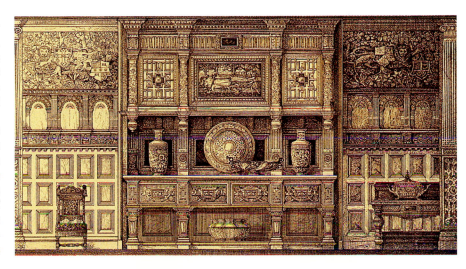

Above: This design is for a recessed sideboard in the Victorian Renaissance manner which was made for the prestigious Leeds furnisher Marsh, Jones & Cribb.

Left: A desk that reflects the High Victorian yen for profuse plastic ornamentation.

considerable influence on later furniture designers, such as William Burges, William Morris, Charles Eastlake and Bruce Talbert.

MORRIS, MARSHALL, FAULKNER & CO

The Gothic Revival furniture designed by Pugin began a movement in British furniture design towards simple construction and restrained ornamentation. At the Medieval Court, a feature of the Great Exhibition of 1851 and the International Exhibition of 1862, such pieces were displayed by Pugin, John Pollard Seddon, Richard Norman Shaw and Morris, Marshall, Faulkner & Co (or Morris & Co, as it was known from 1875). Most of the work was decorated with painted ornamentation incorporating scenes from medieval legends, with long strap hinges, large lock-plates (plates protecting key holes) and handles in chased iron or steel. The designers were trying to evoke, but not to imitate, the furniture of the Middle Ages, and they consciously avoided forms and decoration introduced during or since the Renaissance.

William Morris' furniture-designing career began when he rented rooms in Red Lion Square with Edward Burne-Jones; unable to find furnishings to their taste, they decided to make their own. These solid, architectonic pieces of furniture were strongly influenced

Above left: A rosewood centre table by A W N Pugin (c. 1835). This design appears in Pugin's Gothic Furniture *(1835).*

Left: Oak side chairs designed by E W Pugin (c. 1870). The furniture designed by E W Pugin adhered to the principles of simplicity and clear constrauction that had been preached by his father, A W N Pugin.

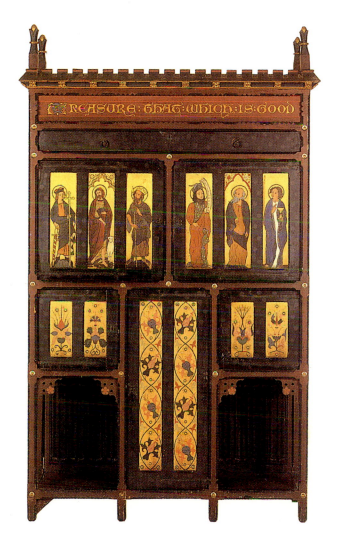

by French Gothic design of the thirteenth century. They were illustrated with Arthurian tales and stories by Dante, painted by Burne-Jones and Dante Gabriel Rossetti. In 1861 Morris and his friends formed Morris, Marshall Faulkner and Co, 'Fine Art Workmen in Painting, Carving, Furniture and the Metals', a 'co-operative' which would produce well-designed and tastefully decorated furnishings.

Walter Crane described Morris & Co pieces as 'representing in the main a revival of the mediaeval spirit (though not the letter) in

Above left: A Gothic-style painted wood cabinet by W Gualbert Saunders (c. 1875).

Above: A painted rosewood cabinet by T E Collcut (1871).

design; a return to simplicity, to sincerity, to good materials and sound workmanship; to rich and suggestive surface decoration and simple constructive forms'. By the mid-1860s, Morris & Co had moved on from its heavy, medievalist furniture and was producing near-copies of traditional country furniture, which appeared to have characteristics adopted from English domestic buildings and furniture of the seventeenth and eighteenth centuries. Rush seating and ladder backs seemed the stylistic equivalent of red-brick chimney stacks and oriel windows. Indeed, the great symbol of Victorian comfort, the deeply upholstered, wing-backed 'grandfather' armchair found its match in the great icon of

Below: A medieval-style oak cabinet designed by J P Seddon, with decorative panels painted by Madox Brown, Morris, Burne-Jones and Rossetti illustrating the honeymoon of King René of Anjou.

the Victorian domestic revival, the rush-seated, ladder-backed 'Sussex chair'.

Much of the furniture produced by Morris & Co was designed by the architect Philip Webb, whose style was characterised by a subtle manipulation of volumes and a refined elaboration of structure. He gradually liberated his work from the domination of the Neo-Gothic style and exploited a wide range of sources, including Japanese furniture forms.

THE OLD ENGLISH AND QUEEN ANNE REVIVAL STYLES

The furniture displayed at the 1851 Great Exhibition was marked by dazzling craftsmanship and stupendous decorative excess, and most middle-class Victorians continued to feel comfortable with lavishly decorated historical pastiches. During the following decade, however, the plainer Old English style came to be favoured, and a little later the Queen

Below: The Green Dining Room, designed by Webb in 1866 for the South Kensington Museum, was a tremendous success. The stained glass and wall paintings were by Burne-Jones, the polychromatic, raised-gesso decoration by Webb, the embroidered screen by Morris and his wife and the piano was decorated by Kate Faulkner.

Right: A marquetry escritoire *and stand designed by George Jack for Morris & Co in 1889.*

Below: A painted wooden cabinet, c. 1861–62. The cabinet is decorated with scenes from the life of St George painted by William Morris. The medievalism of the piece is typical of the furniture produced by Morris & Co during the 1860s.

Anne, both much influenced by architects of the domestic revival, such as Eden Nesfield and Richard Norman Shaw.

The ethos of simple, well-made furniture in the Neo-Gothic or a vernacular style was widely disseminated by Charles Eastlake in his book *Hints on Household Taste in Furniture, Upholstery and Other Details* (1868), illustrated with many of the author's own designs. Eastlake's book assisted the transition from Neo-Gothic to Queen Anne Revival, which became the style favoured by many architects and designers during the 1870s

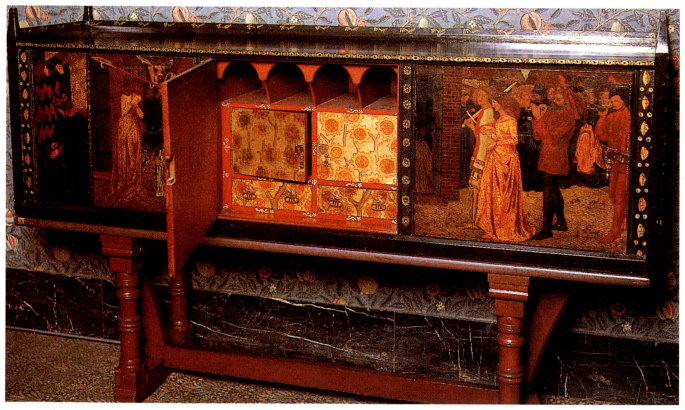

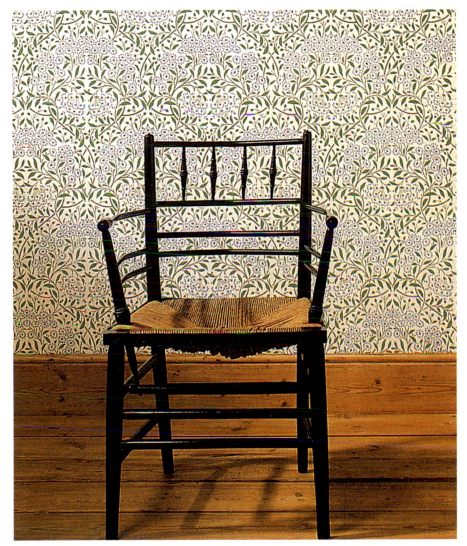

Above: The 'Sussex chair', a traditional, rush-seated armchair of ebonised beechwood by Philip Webb, was a popular Morris design.

and 1880s. Some, such as Bruce Talbert, E W Godwin and Charles Bevan, worked happily in both styles, the main point of their furniture being that it was plainly constructed and generally free of carving and veneers.

The Japanesque furniture designed by Godwin and others shared these features. It was loosely based on the architectural forms of Japan as shown in the woodblock prints which were arriving in the West. Indeed, Godwin is widely credited with the design of the first item of Japanese-style furniture in Europe in the form of a sideboard of 1867. Constructed by William Watt in dark mahogany, with grey paper panels in the style of embossed leatherwork and silver metal details, it is a highly striking piece of furniture. Its resemblance to any known item of Japanese furniture was very slight, but its restrained and geometrical qualities were widely believed to have caught the spirit of Eastern design.

AESTHETIC MOVEMENT FURNITURE

All these various styles contributed to Aesthetic Movement furniture, which was characterised by the extensive use of ebonised wood and was sometime decorated with painted panels or ceramic tiles. Furniture designs by Christopher Dresser included pieces in a wide variety of style, including Greek, Egyptian, Gothic and Japanese.

The furniture that the architect Arthur Heygate Mackmurdo designed for the Century Guild, founded in 1882, was derived from Queen Anne and other eighteenth-century styles. Two pieces, however, had a profound influence on subsequent furniture design and may be counted as important precursors of Art Nouveau. One was a side chair (without arms) which was basically in early eighteenth-

Below right: Although highly decorated, this sideboard by Philip Webb (c. 1862), a founder-member of Morris & Co, reveals the growing concern of the burgeoning Arts and Crafts Movement with plain forms.

Below: A Gothic-style wardrobe, designed by Philip Webb and painted by Edward Burne-Jones with scenes from Chaucer's 'The Prioress' Tale', which was given to William and Jane Morris as a wedding present.

century style but whose fretwork back was decorated with a design of swirling submarine protozoa that looked forward to some French, Belgian and German furniture made towards the end of the century. The other influential piece was a desk by Mackmurdo, based on a Georgian original but formed into uncompromisingly geometrical shapes and the ancestor of many similar pieces designed over

the next three decades in England, Scotland, Austria and the United States.

OTHER NOTED LATE-NINETEENTH-CENTURY FURNITURE DESIGNERS

Furniture designed by George Jack and W A S Benson for Morris & Co during the late 1880s and 1890s was largely based on eighteenth-century forms, although Benson also created

some pieces derived from country furniture.

The Guild of Handicraft, founded in 1888 by C R Ashbee, produced furniture to his design. Loosely Queen Anne Revival in style, Ashbee's designs were often decorated with painted and gilded gesso.

Before setting up their own workshops in the Cotswolds, Ernest Gimson and Sidney Barnsley were both associated with Kenton & Co, an association of architects and craftsmen formed in 1890 to produce furniture of quality. Gimson's pieces were made by carpenters but Barnsley made his own.

The Arts and Crafts Movement is beautifully summarised in Gimson's masterly furniture: simple and solid works, barely decorated and in a functional style drawn from the materials used and the methods of construction. Indeed, the work of both was usually in a 'farmhouse' style: massive, solidly built, with chamfered (bevelled-edge) stretchers (struts connecting legs) and supports and occasionally decorated with inlay or simple, gouged-out ornamentation.

C F A VOYSEY

The designs of the architect C F A Voysey are among the most innovative in the entire history of English furniture. Characteristic features of his work include tall, narrow uprights, broad, flat cornices and large strap hinges with cut-out decoration. His furniture was oak, sometimes stained, and it was made by accomplished craftsmen, such as Arthur Simpson, who subsequently made furniture to his own designs in a style derived from Voysey's.

M H BAILLIE SCOTT

The furniture made by the Bedford firm of J P White to designs by M H Baillie Scott was far more elaborately decorated than Voysey's. Most pieces were inlaid with stylised flowers or birds. The forms, however, were quite simple. When some pieces designed by Baillie Scott for the Grand Ducal Palace in Darmstadt, Germany, were made up by cabinet-makers at the Guild of Handicraft, Ashbee's own furniture became simpler; its decoration, too, was influenced by Baillie Scott's work.

Above: A lithograph by John Dickinson depicting some of the furniture shown at the Great Exhibition.

Left: A bizarre horn stool and chair from the royal family's Osborne House.

Below: A writing desk by A H Mackmurdo for the Century Guild (c. 1886).

CHARLES RENNIE MACKINTOSH

The designs of the Scottish architect Charles Rennie Mackintosh show a virtuosity which is breathtaking, if sometimes self-indulgent. It is easy to understand why his furniture was not well received in England. Simplicity was sacrificed to sophistication, tradition was flouted and scant respect was shown for materials. Many of Mackintosh's designs were parodies of traditional types of furniture. For instance, his ladder-back chair has an exaggeratedly high back, with its narrow uprights ridiculously close together.

His sculptural designs for furniture were enigmatic and highly aesthetic. The furniture was made from various woods, including oak, cypress, pine and mahogany, which were rarely left untreated: they were either French-polished, stained, ebonised or decorated with symbolic motifs, mother-of-pearl and ivory inlays and painted – all anathema to English Arts and Crafts' thought.

MANUFACTURED FURNITURE

Around the turn of the century, several manufacturers produced furniture in a style often called 'quaint' by contemporaries and loosely based on the work of Voysey, Mackintosh and other Arts and Crafts Movement designers. Liberty & Co made stained oak furniture often decorated with *repoussé* (embossed by hammering from within) copper panels and fruitwood, metal and mother-of-pearl inlays. Another firm, Wylie & Lochhead of Glasgow, produced furniture in style that was influenced by Mackintosh, although without his wilder idiosyncrasies.

Left: Oak side chairs by C F A Voysey, 1898. Their high backs, with their extended verticals, and the heart-shaped cut-outs in the splats are typical of Voysey's furniture design.

Below left: An oak cabinet by C F A Voysey.

Below: An oak wardrobe in the Queen Anne style by Gilbert Olgilvie for the Guild of Handicraft, the co-operative group of artist-craftsmen founded in 1888.